SOCIAL JUSTICE WITHOUT SOCIALISM
by John Bates Clark
originally published 1914

based on public domain text.

IT is currently reported that the late King Edward once said, "We are all Socialists, now": and if the term "Socialism" meant to-day what His Majesty probably meant by it, many of us could truthfully make a similar statement. Without any doubt, we could do so if we attached to the term the meaning which it had when it was first invented. It came into use in the thirties of the last century, and expressed a certain disappointment over the result of political reform. The bill which gave more men the right to vote did not give them higher wages. The conditions of labor were deplorable before the Reform Bill was passed and they continued to be so for some time afterwards. A merely political change, therefore, was not all that was wanted, and it was necessary to carry democracy into a social sphere in order to improve the condition of the poorer classes. The term "Socialism," therefore, was chosen to describe a play of forces that would act in this way on society itself, and was an excellent term for describing this right and just tendency. The name was quickly adopted by those with whose practical plans most of us do not agree; but its original idea was democracy carried into business, and at present that is the dominant tendency of all successful parties. For six months we have been living under what may be called "triumphant democracy," not because the Democratic Party has beaten its rivals and come into control of the Government, but for a much deeper reason, namely, that a democracy carried into industrial life is the dominating principle of every political body that can hope for success. Every party must show by its action that it values the man more than the dollar. To this extent we are all democrats and wish the Government to act for the people as well as to be controlled by the people.

When we differ, it is in deciding on the means to carry out our common purpose; and here we differ very widely. Some would use the power of the State to correct and improve our system of industry, and these constitute a party of reform. Others would abolish that system and substitute something untried. For private capital they would put public capital and for private management, public management—either in the whole field of industry or in that great part of it where large capital rules. These are Socialists in the modern and current sense of the term.

One difference of view which was formerly very sharp is now scarcely traceable. Every one knows that we must invoke the aid of the State in order to make industry what it should be. The rule that would bid the State keep its hands off the entire field of business, the extreme *laissez-faire* policy once dominant in literature and thought, now finds few persons bold enough to advocate it or foolish enough to believe in it. In a very chastened form, however, the spirit that would put a reasonable limit on what the State shall be asked to do happily does survive and is powerful. It seeks a golden mean between letting the State do nothing and asking it to do everything. It is this plan of action that I shall try to outline, and it will appear that even this plan requires that the State should do very much. Under an inert government the industrial system would suffer irreparably.

The thing first to be rescued is competition—meaning that healthful rivalry between different producers which has always been the guaranty of technical progress. That such progress has gone on with bewildering rapidity since the invention of the steam engine is nowhere denied; and neither is it denied that competition of the normal kind—the effort of rivals to excel in productive processes—has caused it. It has multiplied the product of labor here tenfold, there, twentyfold, and elsewhere a hundredfold and more.

This increased power to produce has rescued us from an appalling evil. Without it, such a crowding of population as some countries have experienced would have carried their peoples to and below the starvation level. Machinery now enables us to live; and if world-crowding were to go on in the future as it has done, and the technical progress should cease, many of us could not live. Poverty would increase till its cruelest effects would be realized and lives enough would be crushed out to enable the survivors to get a living. Of all conditions of human happiness, the one which is most underestimated is progress in power to produce. Hardly any of those who would revolutionize the industrial State, and not all of those who would reform it, have any conception of the importance of this progress. It is the *sine qua non* of any hopeful outlook for the future of mankind.

I am to speak, however, of *justice* in the business relations of life, and it might seem that this shut out the mere question of general prosperity. The most obvious issue between different social classes concerns the division of whatever income exists. Whatever there is, be it large or small, may be divided rightly or wrongly; but I am not able to see that the mere division of it exhausts the application of the principle of justice. While it is clearly wrong for one party to plunder another, it is almost as clearly wrong for one party to reduce the general income and so, in a sense, rob everybody. A party that should systematically hinder production and reduce its fruits would rob a myriad of honest laborers who are ill prepared to stand this loss and have a perfect right to be protected from it.

Every man, woman, and child has a right to demand that the powers that be remove hindrances in the way of production, and not only allow the general income to be large and grow larger, but do everything that they possibly can do to make it grow larger. It is an unjust act to reduce general earnings, even though no one is singled out for particular injury. On this ground we insist on trust legislation, tariff reform, the conservation of natural resources, etc. I am prepared to claim that it is in this spirit that we demand that private initiative, which has given us the amount of prosperity that we have thus far obtained, shall be enabled to continue its work without being supplanted by monopoly. In a general way I should include public monopoly as well as private among the things which would put a damper on the progress of improvement and lessen the income on which the comfort of laborers in the near future will be dependent. Monopoly of any sort is hostile to improvement, and in this chiefly lies the menace which it holds for mankind.

It is a fairly safe prediction that, if a public monopoly were to exist in every part of the industrial field, the *per capita* income would grow less, and that it would be only a question of time, and a short time at that, when the laborers would be worse off than they are now. Though, at the outset, they might absorb the entire incomes of the well-to-do classes, the amount thus gained would shrink in their hands until their position would be worse than their present one. They would have pulled down the capitalists without more than a momentary benefit for themselves and with a prospect of soon sinking to a lower level than as a class they have thus far reached.

The impulse to revolutionize the system comes from the belief that it is irreclaimably bad. The first thing to be done is to see how much reclaiming the system is capable of; and the only sure way to test this question is to use all our power in the effort to improve it. When all such efforts shall have failed, it will be time for desperate measures.

Our industrial system has many faults:—here we are happily agreed. It is the inferences we draw from this fact that are different. The one that I draw is like one which is recorded in a famous case in antiquity. When the Macedonian armies seemed about to overwhelm Greece, Demosthenes encouraged the Athenians by this very sound bit of philosophy: "The worst fact in our past affords the brightest hope for our future. It is the fact that our misfortunes have come because of our own faults. If they had come when we were doing our best, there would be no hope for us." Now the evils of our own social system which result from mistakes or faults are just such a ground of hope. Every such evil which can be cited describes one possible reform, and the longer the list of evils, the greater is the sum total of gain which we can make by doing away with them. If we cite them all *seriatim*, what impression shall we get? Will it merely show how badly off we are? Will it make us despair for our future? On the contrary, it should fill us with hope for the future. We start from the fact that we have thus far survived in spite of the faults. The worst off among us is above starvation and most of us are in a tolerable state. If we can remove the evils that exist, we shall make our state very much more than tolerable. The greatness of the evils measures the gain from removing them. Every single one that is removed improves the status of our people. We can take, as it were, a social account of stock, measure our present state, measure the extent to which we can improve it by putting an end to one bad influence, count the number of such bad influences, and so get an estimate of the gains of carrying out a complete reformatory programme. It will show an enormous possibility of improvement.

In the struggle for reforms we have the great middle class with us. All honest capitalists, great and small alike, are natural allies of honest labor, and they are interested mainly in the same reforms as are the members of the working-class. If we recognize a necessity for a struggle of classes, it is not one that marshals labor against all wealth. The contention is rather between honest wealth allied with honest labor, on the one hand, and dishonest wealth on the other; and in a contest so aligned, victory for the former party means social justice.

There is a preliminary reform to be carried through as a condition of securing most of the others. Who can estimate the benefit which would come from merely making our Government what it purports to be— government by the people? The initiative, the referendum, the recall, the short ballot, direct primaries, and proportionate representation are all designed to transfer power from rings and bosses to the people themselves. If they actually do it, as sooner or later those or kindred measures probably will, they will so far restore the democracy of our earlier and simpler days as to make us look back on the rule of rings and bosses as on a nightmare of the past. When the Government is thus really controlled by the people we can count on having its full power exerted for them.

What are a few of the things that we shall then try to get?

The working day is too long. In some occupations it covers far too many hours, and in most occupations it covers more than it ideally should. There are doubtless some industries in which hours might be reduced with no lessening of wages, because profits are large enough to bear some reduction. In these cases a strong union might get either more pay for a day of the present length or the present rate for a shorter day. A universal reduction of the period of labor would have to mean a reduction of the product of industry, and without immediate improvements in method of production it would entail smaller wages. Improvements, however, might soon obviate that necessity. With machinery growing more and more efficient, the day may be shortened with no diminution of wages; and the natural effect of increasing power to produce has always been some shortening of labor-time coupled with some enlargement of pay. Within the last one hundred years the period of daily labor in some types of manufacturing has come to cover only a little over one third of the twenty-four hours, instead of more nearly two thirds; while the earnings have become much larger than they were at the beginning of the period. Normally this progress should continue, and long before the dawn of the twenty-first century we should see work still less severe, less prolonged, and better paid. Where, as in some departments of steel-making, labor in two shifts continues through the twenty-four hours, there is a chance to make this gain without appreciable waiting; and elsewhere it should be possible to make it without waiting for the twenty-first century to come much nearer than it is.

Dangerous and injurious occupations still continue; and our country is slower than others in remedying this trouble. Many safeguards that are easily obtainable are neglected. Protection for the workers and indemnities for injuries when they occur can be insured by well-made laws, properly enforced. Sanitary regulations and pure-food laws need to be strengthened and more fully enforced.

Our protective tariff bears heavily on the poor man. His wardrobe contains little or nothing that is made of wool, and he may well sigh for the mixed cotton and shoddy of earlier days. Our import duties, which do, indeed, try to spare his dinner-pail, should be made to spare his wardrobe and the modest comforts of his life.

Commercial crises still occur and are followed by hard times; and while a really wise reform of money and banking would not wholly prevent them, it would greatly mitigate their severity.[1]

Emergency employment is desperately needed when hard times come. European Governments excel our own in providing it, but it is entirely possible to adopt their methods and improve on them.

Our natural resources have been wasted in a prodigal way. Forests have been recklessly cut, fires been invited and the soil itself has been sacrificed. Natural gas and oil have been burned with no regard for the future. Coal and other minerals have not been husbanded. It should be possible for us to cease to play the spendthrift with the patrimony that nature has given to us.

We have the beginnings of a parcel post, but we need a more highly developed one that will come nearer to the standards maintained in other countries. With it we need telephone and telegraph systems that can be universally used.

In our larger cities, we are struggling to get rapid transit and shall have to continue the struggle; but we ought to have, with urban railroads, subways, and the like, measures that would reduce the amount of traveling that has to be done between homes and places of labor. A free use of the principle of "eminent domain" would make it possible to acquire land for carrying out any policy of general beneficence, and that, too, without robbing the owners of it. By resorting to this measure much of the manufacturing which exposes great cities to imminent danger of conflagration might and should be moved bodily to outlying districts.

Of all industrial abuses of the past the cruelest has been the crushing of the life of young children by hard and prolonged labor. We are making headway in removing this evil, but much still remains to be gained; and a vast amount is to be gained by a comprehensive policy for improving the status of working-women.

Social justice demands some effective means of getting legal justice. We have courts, certainly. Do they give the service that we need and, in particular, do they give it to the poor? We do not here impugn the motives of judges. Generally speaking, they are honest; but the whole system of court procedure is hampered by detailed statutes and technical rules, that mean an amount of cost and delay which in itself is the very quintessence of injustice. A citizen is offered a choice between submitting to the wrong inflicted by a fellow-citizen and accepting the wrong inflicted by a dilatory and crushingly costly legal procedure. We probably excel some nations in the rightfulness of the decisions we can get if we live long enough and have money enough to get them; but there are few civilized nations that do not excel us in the rapidity and cheapness of the process. A Chinese student in Columbia University served, during the first year of his residence in New York, as judge of Chinatown, and, by giving up only the Saturday evening of each week to the service, he settled the disputes which arose between Chinese residents. As he was learned in the principles of Confucius, I doubt not he settled them justly, and many a time in that same city I have sighed for his services for native Americans.

The line of division between labor and capital ought not always to be the sharp boundary that it is. Labor should be enabled to acquire a modest share of capital and to invest it securely. Protection for small investments is urgently needed, and would do much to change a proletariat into an independent working-class. This is an essential feature of the social system we wish for and work for. The man who hereafter shall correspond to Longfellow's "village blacksmith" will perhaps be the owner of a hundred shares in some corporation. In agriculture small holdings may always survive; but there may be large ones also, and in that case the farmer of the future may have either five acres and a hoe, or forty acres and a mule, or a hundred and sixty acres and a reaper, or an undivided share in a thousand acres and a traction engine.

If we could carry through even the reforms thus far enumerated, it would make us feel as if we had been lifted from a slough and placed on a plateau abounding in air and sunlight; but if we stopped with this, we should leave much to be desired. There are still more pressing measures to be enacted.

Nearly the greatest evil we are facing is monopoly. This is not the universal view. Though there are few who approve of monopoly, there are those who regard it with toleration and think that, if we accept it and regulate prices under it, we shall fare sufficiently well. As yet, it is in an incipient stage of development and has by no means revealed its full power for evil. If we let it grow freely, we shall find later what it is capable of. Wise measures, adopted even now, will come early enough to prevent it from ever growing to maturity.

With the steel trust, the Standard Oil trust, and other combinations before our eyes, it seems an absurdity to speak of monopolies as being in an incipient stage. Is it possible that anything whatever which these great combinations represent can be nipped in the bud? Are they not already in the fullest flower, and big and mature as they are ever likely to be? The companies themselves, with their vast material plants, certainly are so. What we are talking about, however, is not the mere size of the companies, but *the element of monopoly that is in them*. Have they such a power that they can safely charge anything they please for their products? Is it as though they were licensed by the Government to be the sole makers and vendors of their special wares? Business men know that this is not the case; and that something puts a check on their action. They can make their prices higher than they should be—higher than it is for the interest of the country to have them; but they cannot make them as high as they would be under a real and secure monopoly. The point I am making is that we can destroy such monopolistic power as they have. We can liberate competition, which has, in the main, afforded reasonable prices, and has also guaranteed that progress which is indispensable for maintaining a human life that is worth living. It is to-day the only means of insuring a constantly increasing power over nature—an ability to turn out, in greater and greater abundance, the things which make life comfortable.

These combinations now possess a power which it is highly perilous to let them keep. They can disable their rivals by foul play, which would be impossible under proper rules of the ring. By securing control of raw materials, by selling goods below cost in the territory where a small rival is operating and keeping up the prices everywhere else, by forcing merchants to boycott independent manufacturers, by getting, in spite of laws and commissions, some advantages from railroads, and by other similar practices, they can drive competitors out of business. Yet every one of these practices can be defined and prohibited, and resorting to any of them can be, if not wholly prevented, at least made so perilous that the practices will become extinct.

It is possible to give to every competitor a fair field and no favor, and, in so doing, to infuse again into the industrial system the life and vigor which competition guarantees. This and only this will insure that progress in production itself which is the *sine qua non* of future comfort. It may then be expected that inventions will continue, that machines will become more perfect, and that the power of society to pay wages will grow larger. Labor will then be the heir of the centuries, and under proper laws can claim and get its inheritance. If the world crowds itself fuller and fuller of population and progress at the same time stagnates, nothing can prevent an increase of poverty unrelieved by any bright outlook. Technical progress, power to make two blades of grass grow where one grows now, and to do it in the various departments where men labor, is the sole condition of a sound hope for the future of the wage-earner. It will be as necessary under Socialism as under the present system; but under Socialism it will be difficult to get. In so far as it is possible to judge, it depends on the preservation of normal competition in the general economic field.

Leaders of the Industrial Workers of the World have recently announced an intention of forcing the hours of labor downward from ten hours per day to eight, six, and finally, four, while at the same time the pay will be forced up in a more or less corresponding ratio. They have also announced an intention of making capital useless to its owners, by crippling its productive power, and so making it easier to seize it. It goes without saying that a four-hour day and high wages can never come by a war which destroys most of the income to be divided. Make the figures more moderate and allow time enough for it, and it may be made to come by the diametrically opposite plan of making industry more and more fruitful. The ten-hour day succeeded the twelve- or fourteen-hour one of former times in exactly that way.

The division of the social income is of vital importance as well as the general size of it. I have claimed for the regulation of monopoly that it is nearly the greatest of possible reforms. Perhaps the very greatest is a change in the mode of adjusting wages. They are fixed at present in a rough-and-ready way, though not without some reference to what labor produces and what employers can pay, and not, therefore, without the action of a principle which makes, in a powerful way, for justice. Any method, however, which involves many strikes and lockouts, is bad economically and worse morally. The contests are always costly, and they easily run into violent warfare; but underneath all these struggles and the hates and horrors that result, there is working, if we will see it, a law that makes for peace founded on justice. It tends in the direction of a fair division of products between employers and employed, and if it could work entirely without hindrances, would actually give to every laborer substantially what he produces. In the midst of all prevalent abuses this basic law asserts itself like a law of gravitation, and so long as monopoly is excluded and competition is free,—so long as both labor and capital can move without hindrance to the points at which they can create the largest products and get the largest rewards—its action cannot be stopped, while that of the forces that disturb it can be so. In this is the most inspiriting fact for the social reformer. If there are "inspiration points" on the mountain-tops of science, as well as on those of nature, this is one of them, and it is reached whenever a man discovers that in a highly imperfect society the fundamental law makes for justice, that it is impossible to prevent it from working and that it is entirely possible to remove the hindrances it encounters and let it have the first play. Nature is behind the reformer, often unseen, always efficient, and, in the end, resistless. To get a glimpse of what it can do and what man can help it do is to get a vision of the kingdoms of the earth, and the glory of them—a glory that may come from a moral redemption of the economic system. It is a redemption that man and nature can together bring about if only man himself is worthy of this alliance.

Differences of mere interest between the various social classes are inevitable. There will never be a time when, in the division of any common property, the mere bald interests of the claimants are alike. When two fishermen own one boat and fish together, each one is interested in taking the whole catch. They divide, however, by a fair rule and live in peace. Any similar division may proceed in harmony if what the parties want is justice. Till recently American workmen have lived with their employers without hating them; and if wages can be fixed now by some appeal to the principle of justice, they can live with them in that way again. This means a better method of adjudicating claims than by a crude test of strength. There is no time to discuss a scheme by which this can be done. I must claim that it can be done, and take the responsibility of proving it when more time is available. There are beginnings of a good method in New Zealand, in Australia, and in Canada, and the point I am making now is that if we get a plan which works well in the United States, we shall save a deplorable waste and do more to revive the spirit of fraternity than we can by any measure ever attempted. Struggles of classes there may be, as there are between buyers and sellers everywhere; but this need not make the parties enemies. Its effects do not need to extend to the heart and character and to put distrust and hatred in the place of confidence and good will. The moral effects of this reform will be the best ones, but the economic effects also will be vast and beneficent.

I am not predicting a complete millennium merely as the result of the reforms I have described. That would require also the moral perfection of the human race. Not a little moral improvement is to be expected as the effect of these measures, but it is too much to claim that they will repress all vice and crime, reclaim all criminals, and give to the race generally a keen devotion to duty. A belief in a State where even this will be realized is deeply implanted in human nature, and Socialism itself might easily get a major premise from it. The syllogism would run thus: (1) A better State is bound to come. (2) It cannot come under the system of private capital. (3) Therefore that system must be abolished. So would we all say if the minor premise were true—"The good State is impossible under private capital." We claim that it is possible and that we can see how to realize it. We can trace the forces which, without revolution, will make work lighter, pay better. We also can make a syllogism, and it reads thus: (1) The present State is tolerable. (2) Every reform will make it better, and there are many to be made. (3) The coming State will be whatever we have wit and energy enough to make it.

Our plea for the justice of the coming system will not convince any man who starts with the assertion that capital ought to have *no* return whatever, and that interest is robbery, and that the men who bring empty hands to the mill should take all the product of it. To most men's instinctive judgment this view does not appeal. The general verdict is that it is right for capital to get something.

If we are fishing together from the shore and I make a canoe which multiplies my catch by five, I have a right to the extra return which my new instrument gives me. If my neighbor asks me to lend it to him and I do so, I deprive myself of the extra product I have been getting by means of it, and it is right for him to pay me interest on the cost of the boat. He can do it and make money by the transaction. If his catch is now five times what it was, he can afford to pay me a part of the extra return and still be better off than he was before.

If my share is still large, other men will make boats and offer them for hire. They will compete in lending them till a modest percentage of the cost is all that any owner can get. The borrowers will then get the major benefit. This implies competition and shows the necessity of preserving it.

If, in lieu of lending my canoe, I persuade another man to take it and fish for me, I shall have to give him more fish than he was originally catching; and the more the boats multiply, the larger the share which will have to be given to the men who are hired to work them, and the smaller the share which will be kept by the owner of any one boat. *Under a normal condition, multiplying capital means in itself higher wages.* Higher wages mean that laborers, in the end, begin to get boats of their own, or shares in boats, and that the laboring-class and the capitalist class are more and more merged. Invention—that is, devising and introducing canoes—and accumulation of capital—that is, active canoe-building—mean for laborers higher pay and a chance to save capital.

Do you tell me that this is a primitive State, an Eden of the past and hopelessly vanished from the present earth; that it is a lost Paradise whose gates are forever barred? The whole point of the economic study of which I have given the briefest outline is that it is practicable to create in complex modern life the most essential condition of this primitive life—its tendency toward justice. In the Scriptures the primitive Eden was a garden, but the New Jerusalem is a city. What we have before us for study is a vast centralized economic system suggesting the city; and we have to see what can be made of it.

It is something extremely good. The late Edward Atkinson was fond of saying that, if improvements are allowed to do their best, the time will come when, as he expressed it, "it will not pay to be rich." The workers will be so comfortable that the care of a great capital will more than offset any additional comfort a man can get by owning it. Grotesquely exaggerated as this claim may appear to be, it was based on serious economic study. There are forces at work which, if they have free play, will carry human life very far in the direction of the State so described, with its comfort, contentment, and fraternity.

That fraternity is possible in spite of sharp contention is clear whenever athletic teams meet and celebrate a game which has been a victory for one and a defeat for the other; and the parties that contend in the great industrial field may be equally brotherly if they play fairly. Foul play always means enmity, and fair play, friendship. The finest possible type of character grows up in the course of keen but honorable rivalry. The noblest manhood that can anywhere be developed would come from competing vigorously in the market and living together as brothers when the contest closes. The beaten man may not enjoy his defeat, but he may act rightly and feel rightly toward the victor. Develop in these economic contests the sense of justice—let both parties seek to follow a rule of right—and men's hearts, at least, will not need to be embittered. You will then see a contest, which, when it is waged with bombs and bludgeons, looks like a Sheol, so changed that it shall open the way to a transformed world and make the hope of a future Eden no day-dream, but a scientific deduction from cosmic law. We may build a new earth out of the difficult material we have to work with, and cause justice and kindness to rule in the very place where strife now holds sway. A New Jerusalem may actually arise out of the fierce contentions of the modern market. The wrath of men may praise God and his Kingdom may come, not in spite of, but by means of the contests of the economic sphere.

Socialism can have no monopoly of beatific visions. It offers much in that direction. It draws a picture of a future State of great riches and general equality; and the picture is glorified by a vision of general brotherhood. To some this seems more attractive than any other which imagination can create. I confess to a preference for a prospect which assures, before all else, the continuance of progress, and shows humanity striving to make forward steps and actually making them so long as the universe shall exist. As between a stationary paradise and a progressive purgatory, I should prefer the latter, for the sake of the permanent well-being of the human race; but what I should choose in preference to either is a progressive paradise. The capacity for further improvement is the essential trait of the best condition now in sight. The reformer can point to his delectable mountains and trace an unending route to and over them, as they rise range beyond range and lose themselves in the distance. Men are, in general, following the route, and each generation advances beyond the point attained by its predecessor. Every step is forward and upward, and the nearest goal will soon be reached and passed. Our descendants will reach a better and more distant goal and then press on to something remoter and still better. Again and again barriers seemingly insurmountable will be passed. The impossibility of to-day will be the reality of to-morrow, and the dazzling vision of to-day will be the reality of the future and the starting-point for still grander achievements.